ELWAY

Text by John Elway

Photography by Marc Serota

Edited by Elise Glading

Photography & Picture Editor:
MARC SEROTA

Editor & Project Coordinator:
ELISE KRIGE GLADING

Designed and Produced by:
RARE AIR
1711 N. Paulina, Suite 311
Chicago, IL. 60622
773-342-5180

Co-Produced & Published by:
EGI PRODUCTIONS INC.,
3901 South Ocean Drive
Suite 16L, Hollywood, FL 33019
Sales and Marketing: Scott Goldman

Distributed by:
BENCHMARK PRESS
A Division of Triumph Books
644 South Clark St.,
Chicago, IL 60605
312-939-3330

4

SPECIAL THANKS TO:
Jeff Sperbeck and Karen LaTorre and CLS Sports
2121 N. California Blvd.,
Walnut Creek, CA 94596

Elway Foundation: Kathy Hatch

Denver Broncos: Jim Sacommano, Sara Gilbertson and the entire
Broncos P.R. Department

NFL: Pete Abitante and NFL Properties: Colin Hagen

Sam's Club: Donna Owens; AMS: Pam Morlett and Tiffany Hanson

Kodak (exclusive supplier of film): Lea Ann Ropes and Tim McCabe

Benchmark: Mitch Rogatz, Peter Balis and Heather Hotaling

Rare Air: Mark Vancil and James Forni

Pat Bowlen and the Denver Broncos organization, Mr. & Mrs. Jack Elway,
John, Janet, Jessie, Jordie, Juju and Jack — the Elway team, Jean &
Aaron Frieser, Dan Marino, Greg Brown, Steven Reich, Chuck Greenberg,
Beth Braley, Jackson's All-American Sports & Rock Bar; Rocky Mountain
News Sam Adams and NBC channel 9 Denver.

ADDITIONAL PHOTOS BY:
Colin Braley: pgs 50 top,66-67,109,110
Associated Press: pgs 26,44-45,54-55,102,103
REUTERS: pg 96
Archive Photos Courtesy the Elway Family: pgs 8-19
College Photos Courtesy of Stanford University: pgs. 20,21,23
Gayton Wampier: pg 98

IN LOVING MEMORY OF:
Mary and Daniel Serota, Beatrice Maggi and Magriet Krige.

To My Family, Friends and Fans,

When I sat down to write the forward for my book, I didn't know where to begin. I have been so fortunate that it would be impossible to mention on one page all the people who have influenced my life. From coaches to teachers, teammates, fans and especially friends, all of whom have had such a profound impact on my achievements. But to all of you, and you know who you are, thank you.

With that said, there is a group of people to whom I must pay tribute and convey my sincerest appreciation — my family. My mom has given constant support, patience and love to my entire family, which in turn has been the glue that has kept us all so close. Her influence on me runs far deeper than any words I'd ever be able to express. My dad, who is my hero, my mentor and most importantly, my best friend, has taught me more about life than any one person. Without them there is no me. I love you both very much.

And to my two loving sisters, Jana and LeeAnn, who have supported me throughout the years and attended more football games than they care to remember, I never could have asked for, nor ever wanted, two better sisters.

The past 15 years probably have been the best years of my life. While most would assume that's because I have been playing pro football, that's not the reason. The reason is because five of the most special people to me have been added to my life during that span. First, and certainly foremost, is my beautiful wife, Janet. She is the love of my life, my better half, and the franchise player all rolled into one. If not for her, I would not have lasted in football for as long as I have. Without her, the Elway clan does not function. There are no time-outs for her, she can't go on injured reserve, and there is definitely no off-season. But all of her efforts have paid off because together we have raised four of the greatest kids (I can brag) in the world. But it's her day-to-day influence on them that has established their foundation and formed a value system that will be with them their entire lives. While Jessie (12), Jordan (10), Jack (8) and Juliana (7) are all very different, they have their own unique qualities that make them special in so many ways. I could talk about them for hours on end, telling story after story of why I love them so much. But if I did we wouldn't have room for the rest of the book, so I will tell them how I feel individually instead.

I must single out one other individual — Broncos owner Pat Bowlen. He deserves so much credit, not only from me personally, but from the entire state of Colorado. The level and depth of his commitment to excellence is unique in professional sports. He was not satisfied with just winning games and AFC Championships, he strove for perfection and didn't stop until he brought our state the Lombardi Trophy. And I have a feeling he's not done yet. Thank you, Mr. Bowlen.

In closing, I must thank the people of Colorado, who have supported me from the shaky beginning (like in my rookie year when I lined up for a snap behind the guard) all the way to the Super Bowl victory. At times we weren't sure if we would get there, but you kept the faith, and on January 25, 1998, you made the journey all that more satisfying.

Thank you all for allowing me to be the most fortunate person in the world!

Most sincerely,

John Elway 7

CHAPTER ONE

8

THE BE

GINNING

I was born into an ATHLETIC FAMILY
on June 28, 1960, in Port Angeles, Wash.

My father, Jack, was an outstanding high school and college quarterback, who became a great coach. He joined the professional ranks as a pro scout for the Broncos in 1993. My mother, Jan, played high school basketball and volleyball. My grandfather, Harry Elway, was a semi-pro quarterback in Altoona, Penn.

12

From an early age, ATHLETES WERE MY HEROES, but my parents were my ROLE MODELS.

They encouraged me and helped me to develop my skills. I've always respected what my dad said about sports and technique

I liked the fact I was always around the game of football. We moved around quite a bit because of my dad's occupation as a football coach, but since I can remember, we always looked forward to Saturdays, to go to the games or listen to them on the radio. To me, it was great because I enjoyed being around the competitiveness.

My dad traveled a lot, especially during recruiting season, and my mom worked hard taking care of three little kids. She handled it very well. She is a wonderful mother - loving, yet tough. She was a great disciplinarian and really kept us in line, especially me, I needed to be kept in line.

I used to love playing with my fraternal twin sister, Jana, and our older sister, Lee Ann. We were close in age and I'm sure there was a lot of fighting, but I remember the good times. We were all very competitive, whether we were playing board games, ping pong, diving, ice skating or throwing snowballs.

As a kid, I threw so many rocks out of our neighbor's driveway in Missoula, Mont., that my father had to pay for a load of gravel for resurfacing.

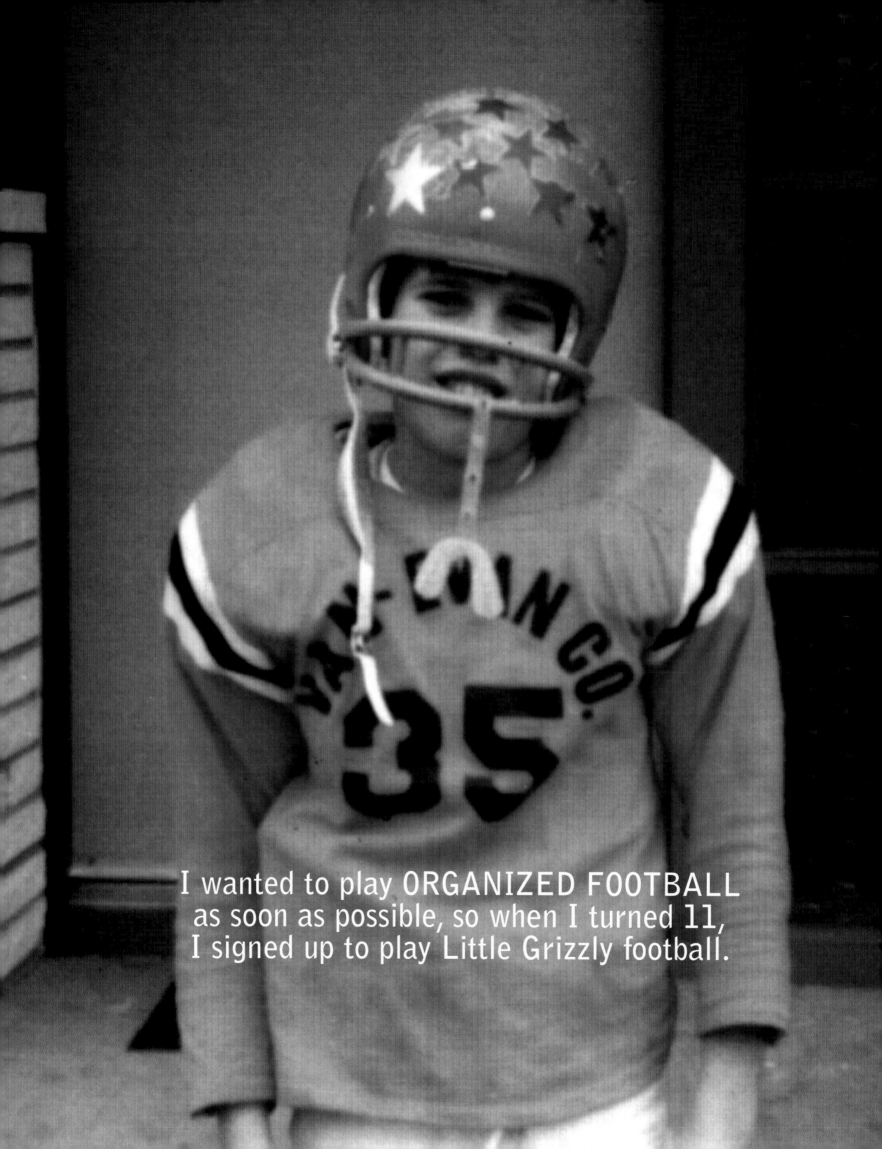

I wanted to play ORGANIZED FOOTBALL
as soon as possible, so when I turned 11,
I signed up to play Little Grizzly football.

But I didn't want to play quarterback. I thought it would be boring to just hand off the ball, so I played running back. My first football season ended dramatically, as our team, Evans Vance Co., won our city championship by beating Stockman's in overtime. After tasting the sweetness of winning a championship, I knew I wanted more.

I learned early about loyalty to my team, and controlling my emotions. My father's philosophy was: Play hard all the time, be a team player and respect coaches and officials. My dad was the biggest influence on my life. Without him, I would not be where I am today. I feel so lucky, he is a great father. He taught me so many lessons in life and I hope my son looks at me the way I look at my dad.

My 8th and 9th grade football seasons were unspectacular and I started focusing on baseball and basketball. My attitude toward football changed the summer before my 10th grade, when we settled in Granada Hills, north of Los Angeles. The high school had a long tradition of winning and coach Jack Neumeier loved the pass. I practiced hard on my throwing that summer, learning to keep my release point as high as possible.

God blessed me with a strong arm, and I spend a lot of time throwing a football and throwing a baseball, so my passing skills developed over time. I never did specific weight training to develop my arm strength, but I practiced a lot especially during my high school years. When the other kids were going to the beach, I would go with a couple of friends and we'd throw 400 to 500 balls a day. The extra effort paid off in my junior year. Our team made it to the semifinals of the city championship. During the fifth game of the next season, I damaged my left knee and needed surgery. We feared that my career would be over, but the surgery was successful and my knee healed well.

The injury made me realize that
NOTHING IN SPORTS IS GUARANTEED.
My dad always used to say, let the future take care
of itself, enjoy each season on its own.

One of MY DREAMS through high school
was to play COLLEGE football.

About 65 colleges recruited me. I decided on Stanford University because of its quality education and tradition of fine quarterbacks. My four years at Stanford produced great memories on and off the field. I experienced thrilling victories and crushing defeats. I made life-long friends, met my future wife and graduated on time with a degree in economics.

I will never forget the first time I MET JANET.

The girl who lived next to me in the dorm in my freshman year was a swimmer and she mentioned Janet, who was an Olympic-caliber swimmer. I was coming back from baseball practice one day and the swimming pool was between the baseball field and our locker room. My friend said, 'Let's stop by the swimming pool, because there's a swim meet today and you'll get to meet Janet Buchan. She's really a babe.' So we got there and Janet and her friend Linda were 1 1/2 laps ahead of everybody else in the pool. That really impressed me. They got out of the pool and I thought Janet looked like a wet rat. When my friend introduced us to each other, Janet wasn't that impressed with me, so it definitely wasn't love at first sight. But, we fell in love as we got to know each other. That was in the spring of our freshman year. She went home to Seattle that summer, but we stayed in contact and dated throughout college. She didn't know whether she liked me, we were just not sure whether it was the right thing, but she kept running back — just kidding. No seriously, I'm so glad that I persisted, because she is the best thing that happened to me.

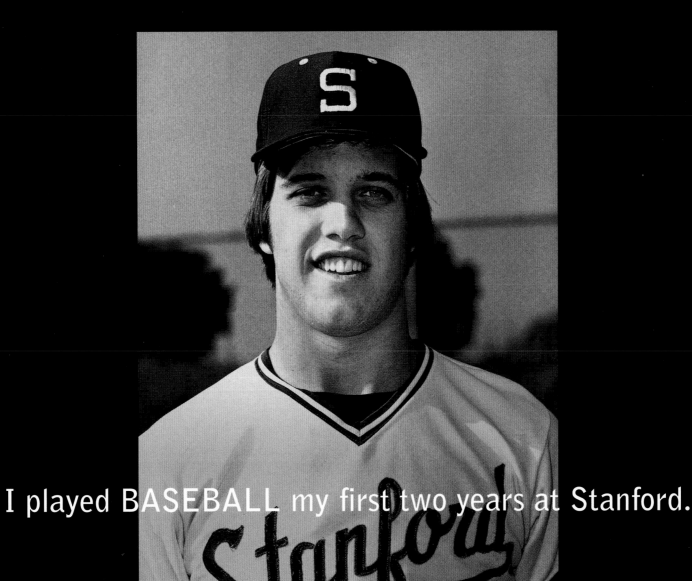

I played BASEBALL my first two years at Stanford.

In 1981 the New York Yankees signed me to play six weeks in Oneota, N.Y., in a Class A league. I hit .318 with four home runs and 35 RBIs in 42 games as an outfielder that summer. I wonder what my career would have been like if I would have chosen to play professional baseball instead of football. I don't think I got close to my potential in baseball because once I got to high school my focus was on football, but I really enjoyed playing baseball. I'm very curious to know what it would have been like to play professional baseball. I had a lot of buddies, who I was comparable with, who went on and played in the majors. There is part of me that thinks that I could have been a pretty good baseball player.

Looking back now, the only regret that I have is that I didn't get to play for my dad in college when he was coaching at San Jose State. It would have been one of the highlights of my life. Ironically, the year I left, Stanford hired my dad as its football coach.

CHAPTER TWO

THE BR

THE DRAFT

I don't think there ever will be another draft like the 1983 QUARTERBACK DRAFT.

It was an honor to be the first one picked in that draft, especially when you look at the guys in that class. It is like a little fraternity and we're all proud that we came out the same year.

The Colts drafted me, but I didn't think my future was going to be with them. I didn't think I could attain my goals with the Colts organization at that time. A standoff lasted for weeks as I considered playing professional baseball, but I knew at the bottom of my heart that I wanted to play football. Finally, the Colts traded me to Denver, which delighted me. The only thing that I regret is not communicating well enough that my problem was with the Colts' management and not the city of Baltimore.

The Broncos' second game of my rookie season was played in Baltimore and death threats were called in against me. I have since received more threats, especially after the Super Bowl losses, but I figure they come from gamblers who lost money. It's really not that bad. It's not like I get something like that every day. It happens, but not that frequently. I guess it comes with the territory. Unfortunately, it's upsetting to my family.

I'm glad the Broncos traded for me. I love the city of Denver. It's a big city with a small town atmosphere. Janet and I got married after my rookie year and we moved to Denver to put down our roots. It's a great place to bring up a family and we really like the people and the area. The Broncos had a great team and we started off having success. We went to the Super Bowl my fourth, fifth and seventh years, even though we didn't get over the hump to win a Super Bowl until later.

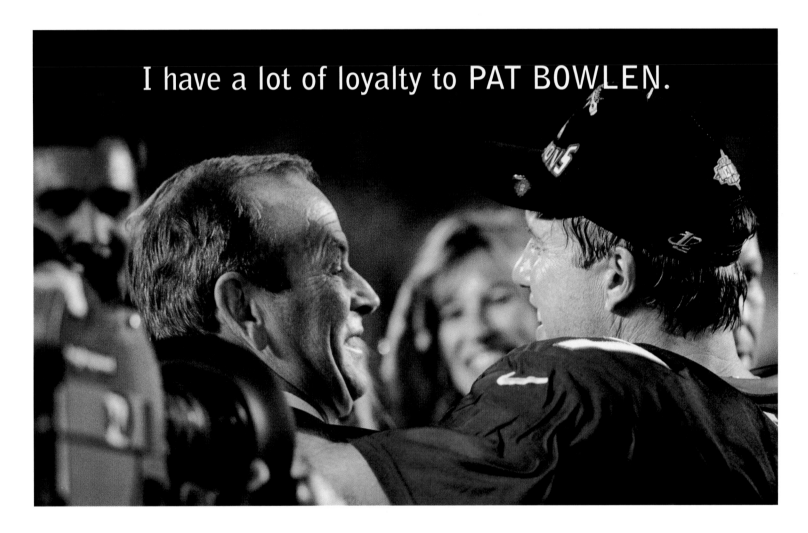

I have a lot of loyalty to PAT BOWLEN.

He is a great club owner because he wants to win as much as anybody and is willing to do whatever it takes monetarily. That's all you can ask for from an owner. I could have left with free agency, but I believe the grass is not greener on the other side of the fence. I had a great opportunity and a great situation, even though we went through some tough times. I want to finish my career with the Denver Broncos.

ROOKIE YEAR

The Broncos signed me to a five-year $5 million deal, making me the highest-paid NFL player before I played my first game.

The pressure was on. I won the starting job in training camp, but felt that role was premature.

I was not ready yet.

On and off the field, the attention was suffocating. I found it difficult to deal with the overwhelming public and media attention

in Denver. During my rookie year, my family and friends were my support team. Janet was my fiancé then but she lived in Seattle that

season. I called her twice a day and she became my emotional cheerleader, thanks to her positive outlook.

COACHES

Some of the joy gradually went out of the game after I turned pro in 1983 and I found myself playing for coach Dan Reeves.

For 12 years Denver's offense reflected Reeves' conservative philosophy. I thought he didn't take full advantage of my passing skills, but I'm not bitter about it. Even though Dan and I didn't have a good relationship, and even though we didn't have the ideal system, we won a lot of great football games and were able to accomplish some good things. Just not enough of them. There's a reason I was always making those come-from-behind victories, we were always behind. Man, that drains you. I hated that, always having to stay close, until it seemed to me like Dan would say, 'OK, go ahead and win it now.' It wasn't just the drive that was draining. I'd be pacing up and down the sideline, waiting for us to get the ball back, wondering how I was supposed to do it. Then I would go home and just lie face down on the couch.

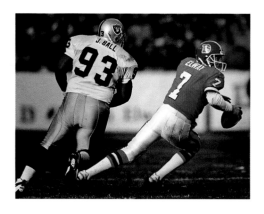

There were times that I didn't like the play
that was called, so I'd just let the rush come in,

FIND A LANE OUT AND MAKE UP MY OWN PLAY.

In a way that style became a metaphor for my career.
Even though those were hard seasons for me, I learned a lot from them.

Coach Mike Shanahan has
MEANT EVERYTHING TO MY CAREER.

He has one of the best offensive minds in the game, if not the best. Getting into his system was a dream come true. I always have a place to go with the ball. It's a quarterback's dream to play in this type of system and to play for Mike and offensive coordinator Gary Kubiak. I really couldn't ask for a better situation.

Shanahan is a great football coach who has had a tremendous influence on my career. We get along so well professionally, and I like him personally. We think alike; we're both very competitive in everything we do, whether it's football, golf, or whatever. I have great respect for him; the way he coaches, the way he works, his drive, his organizational skills. He has made me a better player.

What I like best about his offense is that it's so balanced. We have so many different formations, that it completely confuses defenses — they have absolutely no idea what we're going to do. I love it, it makes it so much easier on me and my teammates.

Mike's approach is very aggressive. He likes to
GET THE BALL IN THE END ZONE.

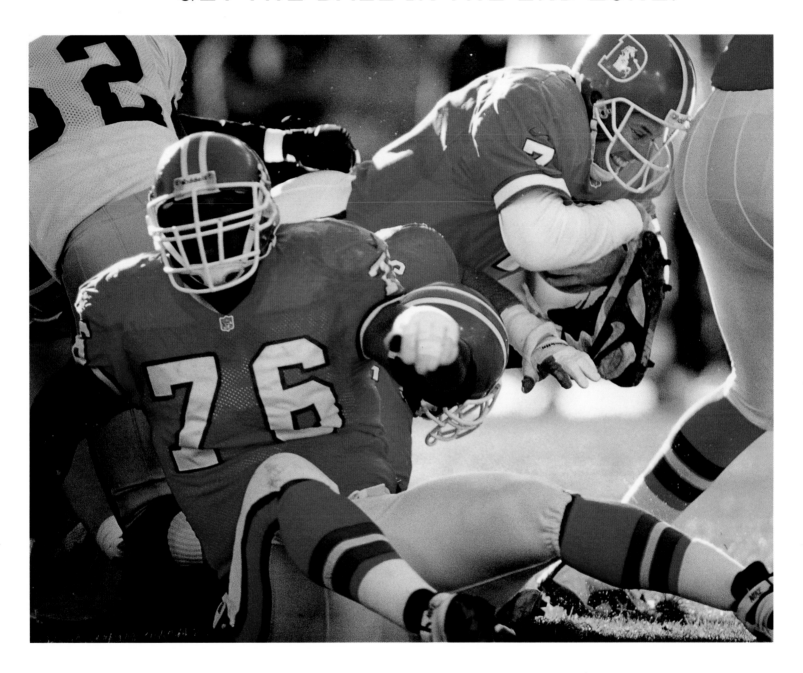

That's my kind of system. My passing skills are much better utilized. It would have been nice to be in Shanahan's offensive system my whole career. But if you go through other systems and do other things, when you finally get to this point, you don't take anything for granted.

3 SUPER BOWL LOSSES

obviously wish I would have won a Super Bowl before, but maybe this was the way it was supposed to be; to suffer through the Super Bowl and playoff losses, to have Mike Shanahan leave and go to a world champion like the 49ers, and see how it's done, then bring that over here to help us. Maybe this was the way it was planned, and how the script was written.

The Super Bowl is the ULTIMATE VICTORY and the ultimate loss.

Losing the Super Bowl is like going from the second best team in the league, to feeling you're the worst team in the league. It is gut-wrenching on everyone involved with the team. The fact that we led at halftime in the first two Super Bowls made it worse.

I remember in our first Super Bowl against the Giants we were just thrilled to death to be there. We didn't take advantage of a lot of opportunities we had in that game. We really played well in the first half, but just got steamrolled in the second half. Against the Redskins, we lost momentum in the second quarter and versus the 49ers we were dominated before kick-off. The 49ers were just so good, we were there on a hope and a prayer. We didn't really have a chance. The game started badly and it just got worse.

The most disappointing game for me was Super Bowl XXII against Washington in San Diego, it took all the wind out of our sails and the roof just caved in. We were up by 10 points and were really doing pretty well. Then we gave up 35 points in the second quarter. That was the biggest bubble burst in my life.

To this day I've never watched a replay of my first three Super Bowls. IT HURTS TOO MUCH.

But those defeats happened a long, long time ago and as time goes by the pain eases and the wounds heal. I've consoled myself that I've walked off three Super Bowl fields knowing that I did everything possible to win. I'm just a cog in the machine. I'm not the machine. You can have a fan belt that works terrific, but if the engine is broken, it's not going to run. Destiny alone can't take you to the Super Bowl — you have to have the players, the coaches, the system, the work ethic, the execution, the commitment — and get some breaks along the way.

Time kind of erases the bad memories. There were several losses, but I'd rather remember the triumphs. The most recent tough loss was the Jacksonville game last year. We also lost to Pittsburgh in 1984 when we were 13-3.

45

I've stopped looking back and saying,

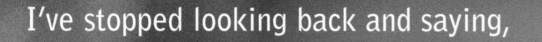

Life is full of could'ves and should'ves and would'ves so I just stopped dwelling on them. You have to play the hand you're dealt and play it the best you can. I've had good hands to play with. All the personal achievements and accolades are nice, but we play to win a championship. You don't play for personal glory, for personal stats. All those numbers mean is that I've been around for a long time and have had some nice players surrounding me. Winning the Super Bowl some day was meant to be.

'WHAT IF...?'

ORGANIZATION

The salary cap, believe it or not, has made us better and put us on the same level with everyone else. It essentially has evened everybody out. Now a team doesn't have to spend the most money to win. With a spending limit, some of the most important factors are your organization and management of the cap. The Broncos organization has been very loyal to me and I owe it to management to be loyal. I had my contract restructured to allow us to reinforce our defense. It was a great move I believed necessary.

Neil Smith was the free-agent PICK-UP OF THE YEAR.

Kansas City has always been a bitter rival and Neil Smith has been there for so long as a great player. I don't know how many times he sacked and hit me. For him finally to be on our side, for me not to have to play against him...he is hitting everybody besides me. I must say I like this set up much, much better.

The only thing I would like to see changed in the NFL is **INSTANT REPLAY** in certain situations. You can really set some guidelines. There is just too much money on the line and it means too much to the players to have a mistake that could be corrected, and **COULD CHANGE THE OUTCOME OF THE GAME.**

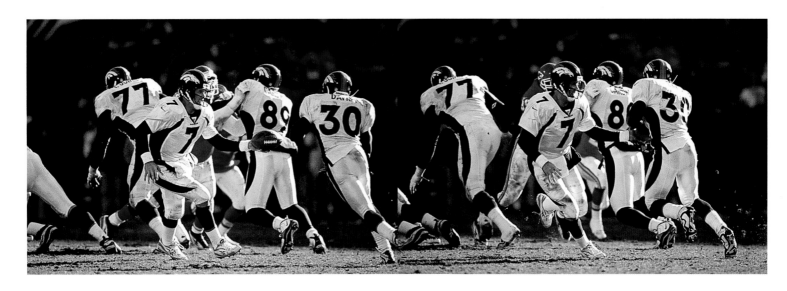

As a player, all you can ask for is to play for an organization that is trying always to get better. If you don't feel like you have an opportunity to win it all, it takes a lot of luster out of the game. At this stage of my career I don't want to play on a team that is going in the wrong direction. A strong team gives you that extra desire to go out and play, knowing you have been given every opportunity to win. In two years, Shanahan has reinstated the club as the AFC's best. He has diversified the offense, putting Terrell Davis at running back and taking some of the pressure off me.

TERRELL is unbelievable.

He is a jewel. He gets better and better, and it makes my job that much easier. He's so strong, and he can run north and south, east or west. Sometimes you don't think he got many yards, that maybe he even lost a yard, but all of a sudden you look up and it's second-and-six. He's a great asset. The bottom line is, he is a terrific player and a terrific person. He handles the spotlight and all the attention so well, keeping his feet on the ground. Ever since we got Terrell, teams have to worry about both the running and the passing game.

Shannon Sharpe is also a guy I always can rely on. I always get great match-ups with him because he's 230 pounds, strong as an ox and he can run. He's the total package. There is nothing he can't do. Rod Smith has the potential to be a great receiver. He is a guy who makes big plays - he does a great job after catching the ball. We got Rod, we got Willie Green in free agency, we got Ed McCaffrey, who had a great year this past season. They're all big receivers too - they're huge targets, and they're great against bump coverage. I'm thrilled with this corps of receivers. Defensively and offensively it is the best team we've ever had.

Talent isn't necessarily the thing that makes a team work — but it definitely helps. You also have to have chemistry, that cama-raderie among the team that shows everybody's willing to jump in the foxhole for one another. We have that cohesiveness on our team.

This is probably the best team I've ever been on, especially offensively. We have the most balance we've ever had with Terrell Davis running the ball. The Denver defense also compares favorably to past years. We're comfortable with it and have a lot of confidence in what it's doing.

I think there is a LOVE AFFAIR between the Broncos and their fans.

That's really special about playing for the Denver Broncos. The loyal fans stuck behind us through thick and thin. Sure they've been upset with us at times, but there is just such great support from a huge area. When we got here there was only football and basketball, and football was the first professional sport in Denver. I think Mile High Stadium is one of the oldest football stadiums in the country, and I've played my whole career in the stadium. I will miss Mile High Stadium, but I know that the Broncos need a new facility. The way economics are nowadays, for Pat Bowlen and the Broncos to stay competitive in the league they need a new stadium. Once it is completed the people will enjoy watching football more in a comfortable new arena.

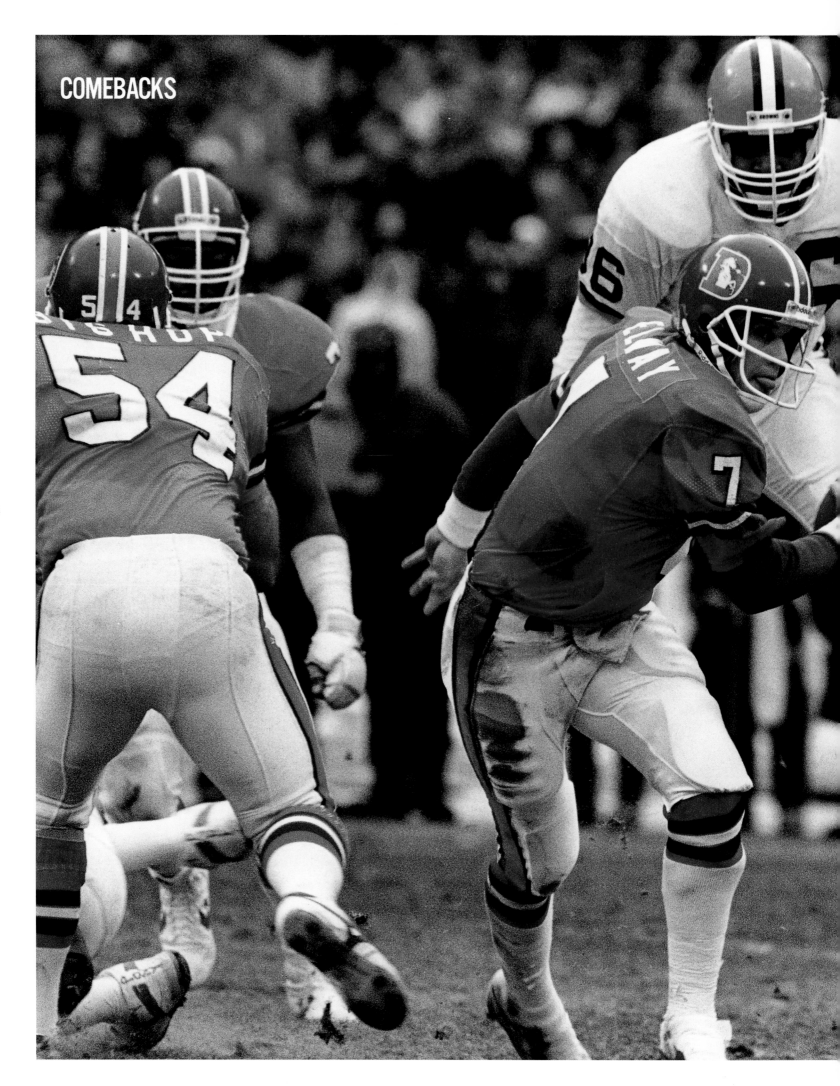

The five most memorable comebacks of my career were: The Drive in the 1987 AFC Championship game in Cleveland, the Drive II in 1992 against Houston, the 24-23 victory against the Chiefs in 1990, another 24-23 triumph in an AFC divisional playoff game against Pittsburgh and the 31-28 victory against the Raiders in 1995.

THE DRIVE WAS MY COMING OUT PARTY. It got me over the hill and put me on the map. It showed I can play well in big games. It established me as a good quarterback in the NFL, showing I could excel in tough situations. That season proved to be a giant step forward, with a trip to the 1987 Super Bowl. I remember the game well. It was freezing as we huddled with 5 1/2 minutes to play at our own 2-yard line. We needed a 98-yard touchdown drive to tie. Considering our last two drives only went for nine and six yards, the task seemed impossible. We all stayed cool, enabling me to lead a 15-play, 98-yard drive over a muddy field and into stiff wind to tie. On one third down I completed a 22-yard pass to Steve Sewell after the snap had bounced off Steve Watson's hip. That was the luckiest play of the drive. On a third-and-18, I passed 20 yards to Mark Jackson. On second-and-10 from the 14, I scrambled for nine yards, then hit Jackson on a 5-yard touchdown pass with 37 seconds left. Our defense held and I directed a 60-yard drive for Rich Karlis' 33-yard field goal for the 23-20 victory, sending us to our first Super Bowl.

55

I wouldn't mind being remembered for staging comebacks. The bottom line is never give up.

IT'S ALL OR NOTHING.

A winner is someone who is able to come back from defeat. Losing is temporary, you can always come back and redeem yourself.

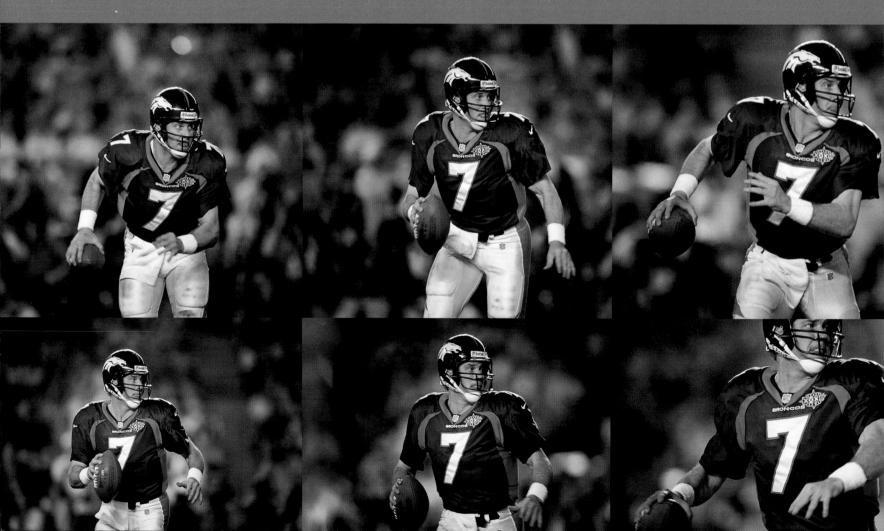

I always liked to come up against the great quarterbacks of my class:
Dan MARINO, Jim KELLY and Kenny O'BRIEN.

They were my contemporaries and we always were competing to see who would rise to the top of the class. You never know

who the next great quarterback will be. I think Kordell Stewart has a chance to be a great player, also Jake Plummer who is with Arizona

and Jeff Lewis a young guy from Denver.

CHAPTER THREE

COMPE

My legacy is that I've always played hard. My strength is not only in my God-given athletic ability, my strength is in my will to win - the competitive fire within me. I believe that my greatest asset, other than Janet, is my competitive nature. I never would quit, until I simply can not play anymore. If there was a crack, I was going to try and get through it and figure out a way to win.

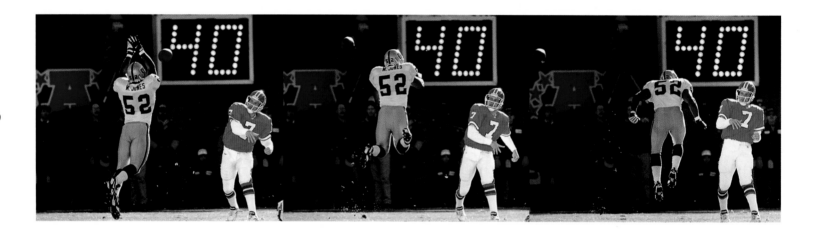

When you give your all, losing is not embarrassing. There can be honor in defeat. Shame comes from failing to try, from giving up and from losing all hope. As long as you do everything you possibly could do. Success is just a comeback away.

THERE IS NOTHING BETTER THAN WINNING,

and that is what life is all about. Winning, and being successful motivates me.
I don't care whether you're a football player, or an executive, or a secretary, you're striving to win,
to be the best that you can be at what you're doing.

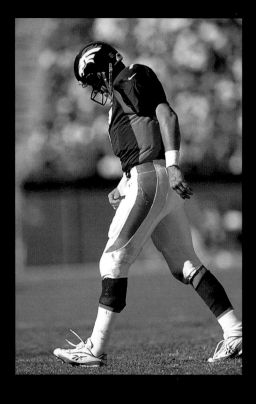
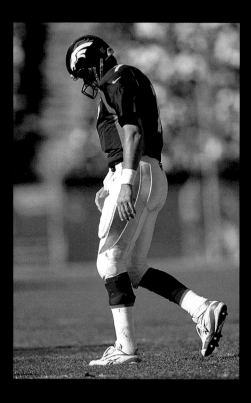
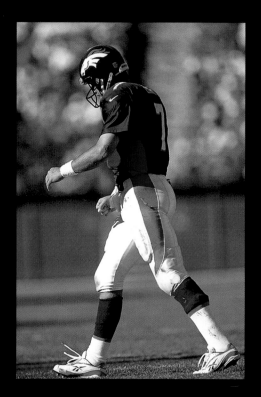

I've made myself stronger over the years. I lift weights regularly and keep workout equipment at home. I try to work on the full body. I work out about two hours a day four days a week during the off season. Each year I have to work out harder and longer to stay in top physical shape, but I believe that age is more of a mindset than a number. At 37, I had one of my best seasons ever.

I don't do all the running around and scrambling, those type of things, like I used to do. But what I've lost physically, I've picked up mentally.

I'M THROWING THE BALL BETTER
and I think the offense I'm in fits me better.

I never used to lift weights until I was in my second year of pro football. Dan Reeves had Roger Staubach call me to talk me into weight training. Staubach was kind of my idol as I was growing up and he taught me the importance of weight training. I started working out then and it has been a big part of why I am able to stay in shape. I'm a strong believer in it. Just as important as the weight lifting, is to be in shape cardiovascularly. When you do get banged up, the muscles bounce back quicker during the year when you're in good shape. A lot of times you get hurt when your muscles are tired. Being in good shape definitely has helped. I run on the treadmill and use the stairmaster to stay fit. Late last season I bench-pressed 275 pounds four times. The extra bulk has helped me to survive collisions.

My worst hit came last season. I didn't see Chris Mims coming, and I stepped into it. I got up immediately, but it hurt. My first response is to get up and not let them know they hurt you, whether I'm hurt or not. One of the key things is to get off the dirt. If they think they can hurt me with one hit, they might play differently. If they know they have to beat on me for a long time before they are going to knock me out, it makes a difference. I tolerate pain well and I'm fortunate to be a fast healer. I also don't want to miss any games. Early in my athletic career, during a game in my junior year at Granada Hills High School, I hurt my left knee just before half-time. I had it taped up and played the second half. We later discovered that I had a completely torn anterior cruciate ligament, and needed surgery. Thirty days later the doctor cleared me to play baseball. My intense desire to win and play has allowed me to play hurt.

I try to avoid getting hurt by using my INSTINCT and my PERIPHERAL VISION for READING and seeing the field.

68

I was taught to play with my eyes and ears open. There is a knack of knowing when you're in a vulnerable spot. I keep my feet moving and see the rush. I also wear protective gear when I play. As a quarterback, your legs are so vulnerable. As you get older, you develop a feel of when people are around your legs. One play, you might have to throw the ball away – even if you have someone open – to avoid an injury.

69

I can hear when a 300-pound defensive end is coming my way. Even in a stadium of 75,000 screaming fans, I can hear the padding feet of an opponent.

I like to hang in there and pretend I don't know they're coming, then they get up speed and go for my head, I can duck them.

Oh, and shadows, especially in domes. I think I've always done it, but I noticed it the other day after a game at the Metro Dome in Minnesota.

With all those lights, your body gives off shadows in every direction. Under a heavy rush I sometimes turn my back to the line of scrimmage, feeling the heat on my body and spinning away from the pressure.

I've been sacked 463 times and I've been crunched countless times more. But I've been pretty lucky and blessed with great health for the majority of my career.

My arm is not as strong as it used to be, but I'm more accurate than I've ever been and I throw with a little more touch. It is better to pick up those two qualities at this stage than to have more arm strength. Instead of being able to wing the ball 80 to 85 yards, I can throw it 65 or 70 yards, which is plenty. During the pre-season in Mexico, I sustained a ruptured biceps tendon in my passing arm. The doctors didn't know what would happen. A thrower had not suffered that injury before. It usually is an injury an offensive lineman sustains. When I came back at the end of that first week, it felt better because before I tore it, it had been partially torn and that had been bothering me. The tear relieved the pressure and the pain went away. My main concern is that my arm is ugly and my wife won't like me as much. Seriously, I'm going to be a little more sore later in life, but it's a sacrifice one makes to do what I do now.

You never really think about your career ending, but when the injury first happened, I did think that this could be it. I was sitting on the bench and kind of had a pit in my stomach, thinking I could have played my last game. For the first time in my life, my whole football career flashed in front of me. The injury caused me to think how soon it all could end, how I needed to enjoy every game as if it were my last, how I needed to make it a game again. This season I've enjoyed it much more, realizing the amount of football I'm going to be playing is running away from me. Injuries make me realize that nothing in sports is guaranteed.

74

SUPER BO

GAME PLAN

Our overall game plan for the Super Bowl was to stay low key and focused. We were 14-point underdogs and no one really gave us a chance, but that just added fuel to the fire. I guess everybody thought we would be underdogs, but it was an insult to be that big of an underdog. Everybody thought the Packers were great, but we just kept our mouths shut and let them talk about how great they are. We felt if, given a choice, we would rather play Green Bay at a neutral site than Kansas City in Kansas City, or Pittsburgh in Pittsburgh. We felt pretty good about our chances of going out there and showing the world just how good we are.

We took a one-play-at-a-time approach. We were so happy to be at the Super Bowl. Defensively and offensively, we had the best team we've ever had. Mike Shanahan put the game plan in early. As we reviewed it the night before the game, Mike and I couldn't wait for the game to begin. Before the other Super Bowls, I really didn't grasp how big they were. But I've never been so ready for a game in my life.

BEFORE THE GAME

I really didn't care that the Packers were favored so much. We knew they were a great football team because we had seen them on film and we knew we were going to have our hands full. Brett Favre is a guy who is a great athlete and a lot of fun to be around. He has a great sense of humor, enjoying life and the way he plays reflects that attitude. He isn't afraid to make the big play and has no qualms about pulling the trigger or making a mistake. He has as strong an arm as I've ever seen and he is in the height of his career now. Defensive end Reggie White has been a great player for a long time and he is still playing at that level. Defensive back Eugene Robinson is also a guy with great athletic ability and instincts. You can't concentrate on one player: You have LeRoy Butler and Gilbert Brown, you have to look at the defense as a whole. We knew we had to play our best game to beat them.

Everything was going by so fast, going 800 miles per hour, going so quickly I didn't even catch a glimpse of the B-2 bombers that flew overhead, just as I was being introduced to the crowd. ALL I SAW WAS SMOKE.

I didn't dream about winning because I wasn't going to set myself up for disappointment. I tried to concentrate on playing a 60-minute football game. I realized the game wasn't going to be won in the first or second quarter. We had to play a complete game. If we won, we would celebrate then. Also, I didn't want to build it up and then have it not be as good as I thought it would be.

I was relaxed and confident. There was so much pressure on me and everybody was saying that this was my last chance. But I just said to myself, 'John, all you can do is to go out there and play as hard as you can and do the best job that you can.' That's what I really concentrated on throughout the game. I never got too worried about being behind, or too happy when we got the lead. I stayed on an even keel.

FIRST QUARTER

I can just imagine how the Packers must have felt coming into the game, as 11 1/2 point favorites and jumping on top of us 7-0 in just over four minutes. We had to answer the bell. I think all drives are important, but when they came out and scored, it was much more important for us to come back and put it in the end zone to stay even — especially with the way we've started in previous Super Bowls.

We charged back on a **10-PLAY, 58-YARD DRIVE** with Davis running in from one

yard out. For the first time in Super Bowl history both teams had scored on opening drives.

SECOND QUARTER

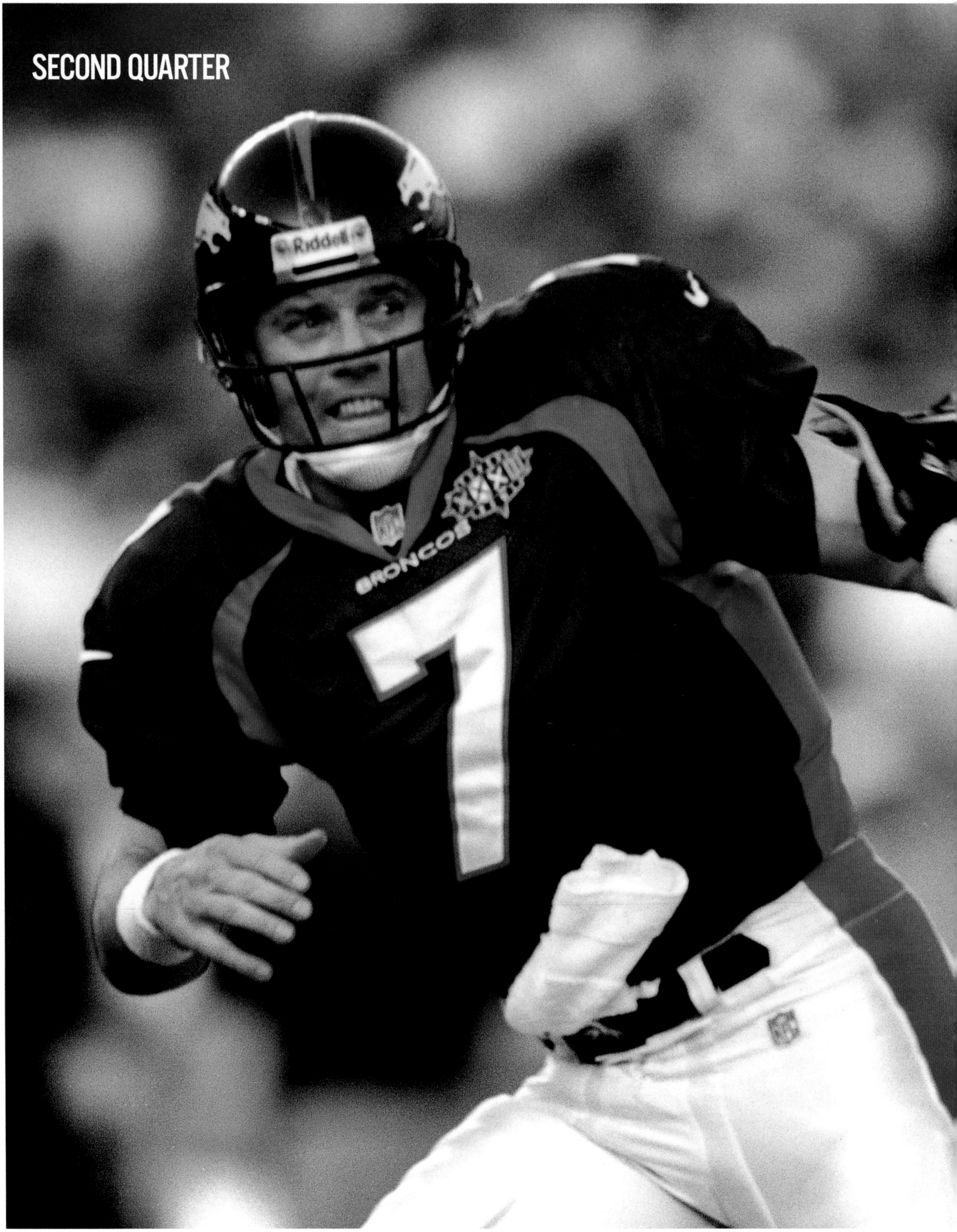

Green Bay's game plan was to send in the safeties and I had Leroy Butler in my face throughout the game. Leroy is a great player and he could really have caused havoc for us. Going into the game we knew that we would have to block him and we had to make sure that we knew where he was throughout the game. He was a key for us in the end. We went ahead after taking advantage of a Packer turnover, cornerback Tyrone Baxton intercepting a Favre pass at the Green Bay 45. On third and goal from the 1-yard line, eight plays later, I faked a hand-off to Davis and ran untouched into the end zone for a 14-7 advantage. Jason Elam kicked a field goal from 51 yards for a 17-7 lead. Green Bay struck back with 12 seconds left in the first half to cut our lead to 17-14.

We had more stats for this game than we ever had. During the week I looked at one of the stats in my playbook and I noticed that the Packers lost three games. Every time they were behind at the half, they lost. So, I stumbled across the stat, and I felt pretty good about that, just hoping the trend would continue. The team spirit was good at halftime. We were happy, but we realized that there was still a long way to go. Everybody stayed focused, we knew it was going to be a long halftime. This halftime was almost twice as long as usual with all the Super Bowl activities going on. So we knew we couldn't get too excited, we had a long wait before we could go out and play the second half.

The chance to be a world champion got the adrenaline going. It was something we had worked for since minicamp in April. Finding the energy was easy, we had to try to settle down, to pull in the reins, not to get too excited.

THIRD QUARTER

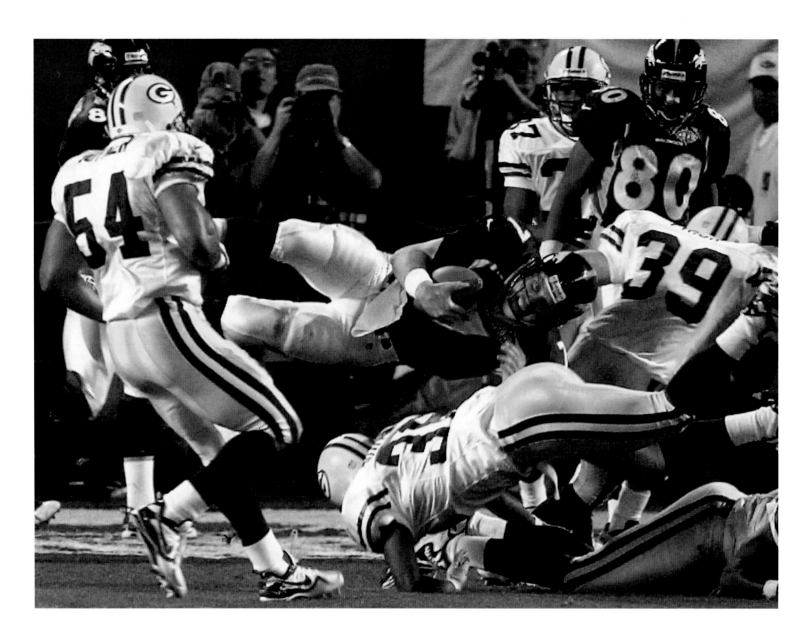

The atmosphere was electrifying and the crowd noise was deafening. It was difficult to hear the plays being called. Ryan Longwell's 27-yard field goal tied the game 17-17 with about 27 minutes to play. I took us back, guiding the Broncos from our 8-yard line to the Green Bay 12. On third-and-six, the heat was on. I took off running rather than slide to the ground, hurdling my body at a trio of Packer defenders, using all of my three-inch vertical leap for that. I went cartwheeling into the air, landing hard for an eight-yard gain. The first down set up Davis' second one-yard touchdown run, and we were leading 24-17.

Suddenly I was on the hot seat —I had been talking about just once being in the position to win when we got to the fourth quarter. We were finally there, and I'm thinking, 'Now let's do something to get it done.' We knew we couldn't turn the ball over very often. That was big at the time. I had two crossing routes and saw Eugene Robinson go across with Eddie McCaffrey. I attempted to pounce quickly instead of taking the safe route, I got a little aggressive there and thought that could be the dagger.

I THOUGHT I COULD SNEAK IT IN
the back side but Eugene made a great play and stopped us. We didn't score any points on that drive.

Green Bay's Antonio Freeman scored his second touchdown of the game and we were tied 24-24. I kept saying: "We need seven points. We can't afford to just get three." I was worried about scoring with time remaining in the fourth quarter, because we had first and goal on 1. I asked about that when we got to the sideline. I said: "Do you want to use some time, or make them use a time out?" If we would have known that we were going to get in there that easily, we probably would have wasted a little bit more time. We would have taken a knee or sneak something, but it turned out fine.

I was just hoping and praying our defense would stop Green Bay on its final drive. Our defense had been playing great all day but Favre is the best quarterback in the league. Still, our defense had made the plays against him. But you're never positive, you're always a bit worried — especially when they have a guy on the field like Brett. When that last ball hit the ground, it was unbelievable. When I saw Brett afterward, I told him that he was even better than I thought he was. He'll be back many times and have many more Super Bowl rings.

On first down, Darius Holland's 15-yard face mask penalty jump started our final drive to the winning touchdown. It helped that our offensive line, despite being the league's lightest, had worn down the Packer defense.

I could not believe how fast the second half went by, we kind of just watched it go by. The next thing I knew, I looked up at the clock, we had the ball, there was 3 minutes and 20 seconds left and we were on the 40- or 50-yard line. I'm thinking, man, this may be our last chance of the year. All I wanted to do is to get a chance to win it.

In my book, Terrell Davis is the best running back in the league - bar none. He showed it again at the Super Bowl. He is always breaking tackles, always going north-south.

When we scored our last touchdown I knew that we were ahead for good. I raised my arms in a 'V' punctuating the 31-24 victory. The feeling was indescribable, three times better than anything I could have imagined.

VICTORY

92

If I would have thought about BEING CARRIED OFF the field by my teammates, trying to imagine what it would feel like, I wouldn't even have been close.

Not only were we the world champions, but to think 15 years of hard work had gone into it. The fulfilling of a goal that you've had for the past 15 years, for me to explain the joy of achieving it, and to put it into words, would be impossible.

When I first saw Janet after the game she was bawling, she was just sobbing and couldn't quit crying. She must have cried for 10 or 15 minutes straight. We hugged the kids, but Janet couldn't even talk. I think it was as hard emotionally on her as it was on me.

That was the ultimate victory, there's no question. To finally come out and show the fans is unbelievable - this is what we play for. I know that I've been labeled The Guy Who's Never Been on the Winning Super Bowl Team. The NFC - AFC thing. You take that for a long time. All of those things we've been answering questions about for the last 15 years, makes it that much sweeter. There's only so many times you can get hit right in the forehead with a fist, but this time we did the punching.

FANS

Winning a world championship is one thing we hadn't been able to do before. The organization has been here four times before this year. It deserved to be here and to win. The victory put the Broncos up there with the elite organizations. The fans have been loyal since 1960, when our team came into existence. The trophy is for everybody in the Rocky Mountain States. So many fans from Colorado have been disappointed so many times. There are no more deserving fans - I'm not just talking Denver, I'm talking the whole Rocky Mountains. There are a lot of people in the Rocky Mountain States who are proud to be Bronco fans.

The fire truck parade was a wonderful experience. It was great seeing the people's faces and how thrilled they were. It wasn't only the joy of fulfilling a goal, but also the joy of fulfilling a dream of so many people and so many Bronco fans. The feeling of giving something back to the fans is great. It is something that they have been waiting for a long time. There is a lot of joy in that. Now they can walk around saying that they are the world champions. Their team is the world champion. They can be proud of being Bronco fans and know that they have the best team in the world.

FAMILY REACTION TO THE VICTORY

It was awesome sharing the victory with my family, and having them there with me. My son and my daughters like watching football, they are old enough to understand the game and could really appreciate the triumph.

MY DAD IS MY HERO and MY BEST FRIEND
and for us finally to be on the same team and
to be able to accomplish this together is — well—
I can't put words to it. He has been my mentor
and the reason why I made it. He's the best.

98

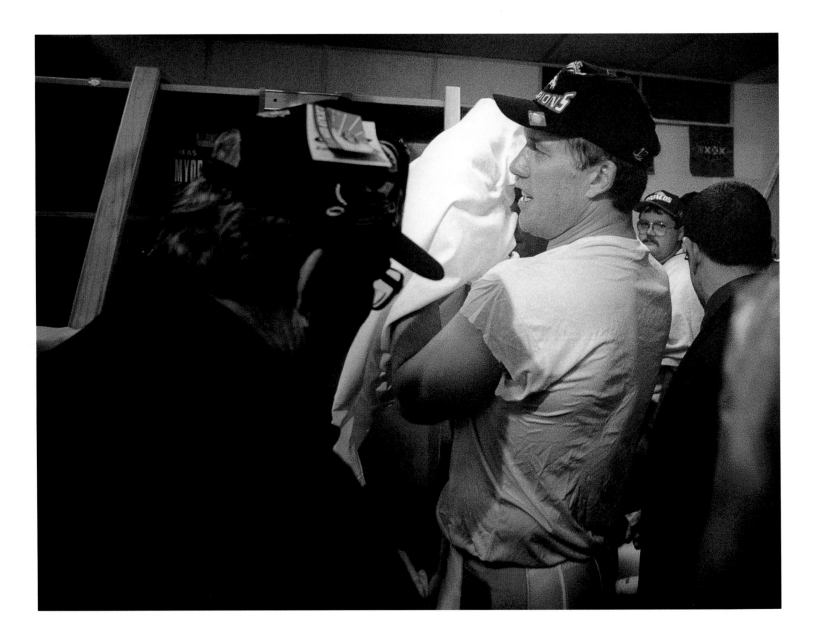

Other than marrying my wife and my kids being born, there is nothing better than winning the Super Bowl. It is extra special

that my kids are old enough to understand what's going on. Before the Super Bowl, I asked my son Jack, 'Do you know what the Super Bowl

is?' He said, 'I know if you win it, you get a ring.' It was awesome having him in the locker room with me after the game and it was funny

when he asked me where the ring is. It was so special, the memory will be with him forever. I think back when I was with my dad, he and I

would go into the locker room, hang out and see the players, that will always be stuck in my memory.

CHAPTER FIVE

100

PERSP

FAMILY

I've learned perspective. You get married, have a family and do different things outside football. Early in my career, football was it for me, my only priority. I used to put all my importance on winning the Super Bowl, but it has changed now. Time is traveling so fast. It is like yesterday when I was 28 years old. Realizing that time flies by, helps me to see things in perspective. I'm blessed with a beautiful wife and four healthy children, Jessica (12), Jordan (10), Jack (8) and Juliana (7).

I was way over my skis when I married Janet. I WOULDN'T HAVE BEEN HERE WITHOUT HER. She didn't like me a whole lot when we first met in college, but I'm so glad that I was persistent.

Janet is instrumental in my success and is equally responsible for it. For me to go and play football the best I can, and to concentrate on my job, and not have to worry about the kids being taken care of is important. Without her helping hand there would be no way to do it.

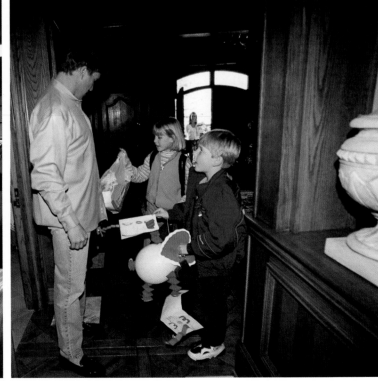

It's fun being a dad. I enjoy football even more because I can go home to my family and get away from the game. My son Jack, is an 8-year-old rookie for the Eagles. They have a pretty good team, even went to their Super Bowl. Jack is the quarterback and he wears a number 7 jersey. Watching him play sometimes makes me wish that I could go back and do it all over again.

My daughters are also athletic. Jessica is very competitive and a hard worker. She really enjoys playing sports. Jordan who is just a little smaller, plays soccer and basketball, like Jessica. Juliana also is going to play soccer, but she is still into Barbie dolls.

My outlook on life has changed a lot during the past few years. I think as you grow older, your outlook changes. When you first get into the league, number one, you want to be successful, you want to make a name for yourself. As you grow as a quarterback, you want to be known as the best there ever was.

Later, you see life more in perspective, and the Super Bowl is NOT YOUR ONLY GOAL IN LIFE.

THE MEDIA

My relationship with the media is good. I've been around for so long and have fielded so many questions from the media that

they can't ask me any new questions. In Denver, the media coverage is intense. There are two local papers competing with each other for the

scoop. Sometimes there are things that go over the line, but I think with maturity you realize that is just the way it is. You have to deal with

the media and you realize you can't control what is said or written.

You become numb to all the attention from the media and the fans. It's not easy to get gas, go get donuts, get coffee. You're

not allowed to be in a bad mood. There are times you just don't want to talk. Probably the hardest thing is raising kids. You are not able to

go where the kids want to go. Usually when you go to those places, there are lots of other kids, and what were the toys become

secondary to me - I become the toy. That makes it tough.

CHARITY

The fame of playing in the NFL has brought thousands of letters and requests from people, many of them from people who need help. We have had the Elway Foundation for about nine years now. We have raised more than 3 million dollars for the treatment and prevention of child abuse. Janet and I are really proud of it. I think when we first started, we got pulled in many different directions. I wanted to make sure that 90 cents out of every dollar that was raised would go to the right place. We had to pick a cause, and because we love children we created the Kempe Children's Center and F.A.C.E.S., both focus on the prevention and treatment of child abuse. We were able to raise awareness as well as money. This also helps me to see life in perspective.

More people need to take a stronger stand to support education. Education is the one area in which we have the ability to make a difference and create a better future. I've provided college scholarships to 72 needy students. I used my Stanford football scholarship to earn a degree in economics, while Janet attended Stanford on a swimming scholarship. Neither of us would have been able to afford it otherwise. My education will last a lifetime, while my ability to play football won't. I want to give others the opportunity to get an education and have a better future. There are so many kids out there who have the intelligence, but not the resources to go to college.

We just want to give these less fortunate kids the chance to live out their dream of going to college. We were able to do that because of the people who support our auto dealerships. We raised $320,000 last year, and it is satisfying to be able to do that.

FUTURE

At this point, I'm not exactly sure what the future holds. I know football will end at some point. I don't know whether I will continue in football. Fifteen years is a very long time. I want to get away from the game a while and think about it. I don't know about retirement. It's tough to know. I will see how I feel physically and will discuss it with my wife. I don't want to wake up on a Monday morning limping and hurting. Before Super Bowl XXXII, I was outvoted in my family 5 to 1 about retiring. You know who the one is.

There never is going to be a right time to make the decision to leave the Broncos and step away from football. I don't think there ever will be a time when I will say that I just don't want to play any more. But, there are times when the negatives outweigh the positives. The soreness for days after the game, the physical work you have to do during the off-season and in season, make the decision tough. There is definitely going to be a void after I retire. Talking to a number of guys who have retired, they say it takes some time to get through it. When they talk about you being old all the time, like they do to me in this business, I have to remind myself that I'm still young otherwise. There is a lot of life after football and I look forward to those challenges. What I will miss on the football side will be balanced by not having to go through the physical stuff I do to play at this level.

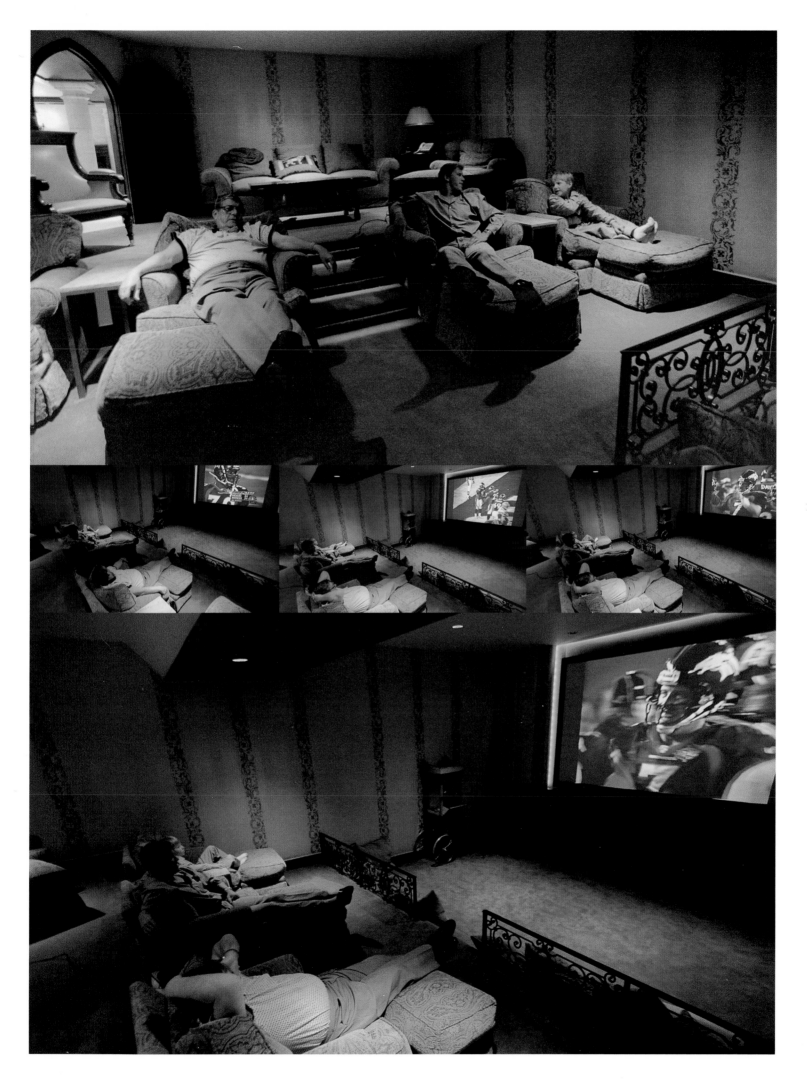

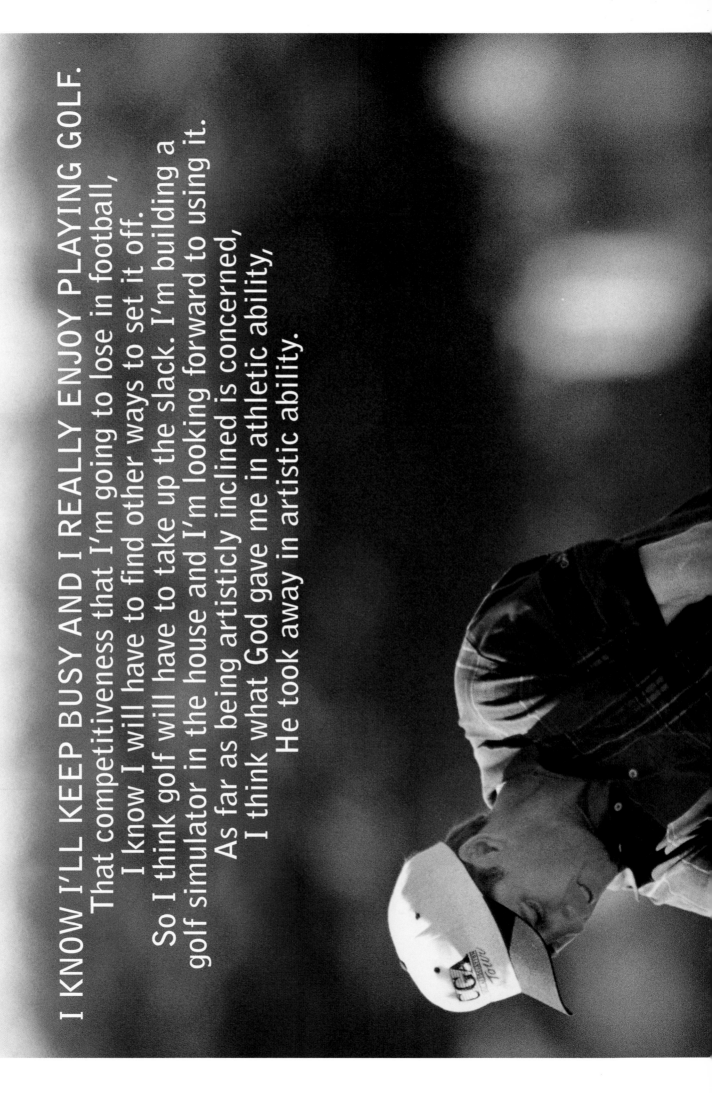

I KNOW I'LL KEEP BUSY AND I REALLY ENJOY PLAYING GOLF.
That competitiveness that I'm going to lose in football,
I know I will have to find other ways to set it off.
So I think golf will have to take up the slack. I'm building a
golf simulator in the house and I'm looking forward to using it.
As far as being artisticly inclined is concerned,
I think what God gave me in athletic ability,
He took away in artistic ability.

114

I'm really not a materialistic guy. I enjoy nice things, but the most important thing to me is my home.

I want a home that is warm and, as the kids grow up, I want them to like spending time at home and bringing their friends over here. Janet did a great job with making our house warm and friendly.

118

I have sold my car dealerships, but I still have a chance to continue to work in the car dealership business and keep an eye on my investment. Politics intrigue me, but I don't like the way the people attack the candidates and scrutinize everything they have done in their lives. That's really a turn-off to me. It is a turn off to a lot of good people, who could make government better. As time goes by, things may change and it may be an option for me.

I can look at myself in the mirror and say that
I HAVE DONE EVERYTHING I could have done in my football career.

I'm at peace with myself and I'm enjoying life. Nobody knows how many next seasons any of us has. Until the last second has ticked in my last game, I always will try for one more comeback.

THE BOTTOM LINE IS FAIRY TALES DO HAPPEN, BECAUSE IN MY LIFE THEY HAVE.

In more than 15 years there have been a lot of ups and downs, a lot of aches and pains and a lot of disappointments, but I think that if you continue to work hard, you know what, if you believe that good things will happen, they will. I have to pinch myself sometimes, because it is unbelievable, and I thank God for that.